Tips
for Teachers
Early childhood

compiled by
PEGGY DAHARB

contributors
JANELLE AXTON
DOROTHY BRUNSON
CHERIE BUTLER
PEGGY DAHARB
LORI FOX
LORI PAYNE
JIM PIERSON
JANE L. SIMMONS

STANDARD
PUBLISHING
Cincinnati, Ohio

Edited by Karen Brewer
Illustrated by Lorraine Arthur
Cover Illustration and Book Design by Sandy Wimmer

The Standard Publishing Company, Cincinnati, Ohio
A division of Standex International Corporation
© 1995 by The Standard Publishing Company
All rights reserved
Printed in the United States of America

02 01 00 99 98 97 96 95   5 4 3 2 1

Library of Congress Cataloging-in-Publication Data
Tips for teachers: early childhood/compiled by Peggy DaHarb;
contributors Janelle Axton . . . [et al.].
    p.   cm.
  ISBN 0-7847-0315-9 (pbk.)
  1. Christian education of children. 2. Christian education-
-Teaching methods. 3. Bible—Children's use. 4. Creative programs
in Christian education. I. DaHarb, Peggy. II. Axton, Janelle.
BV1534.T56   1995
268'.432—dc20   95-6405
                                                        CIP

CONTENTS

NEWBORNS TO 2-YEAR-OLDS

THE CHILD

"Before I formed you in the womb I knew you"
(Jeremiah 1:5, *NIV*).

NEWBORNS TO 2-YEAR-OLDS

Are changing daily and experiencing rapid physical growth

Thrive on movement

Imitate simple sounds

Like words and like people to talk to them

Are learning to trust

Learn through sucking, touching, and looking

Are dependent for all needs, and cry to make needs known

Have favorite toys, books, songs, etc.

Spiritual Understanding

Caretakers teach love.
Jesus loves me.
The Bible tells about Jesus.
God made trees, animals, food, and me.

2- AND 3-YEAR-OLDS

Have short attention spans and need rotated activities

Have one-track minds but can be distracted

Are determined and shouldn't be discouraged

Imitate others, so good examples are important

Are self-centered

Can't sit still

Need a lot of physical play and space

Learn by actual experience

Have unlimited questions, especially "Why?"

Are uninhibited and need protecting

Play independently, side by side

Are learning self-help skills

Spiritual Understanding

God made and cares for the world.
God made and cares for people.
Jesus is my friend.
Jesus is God's Son.
Jesus was a baby, a boy, and a man.
The Bible is a special book.
The Bible tells about God and Jesus.

> The Bible is God's true Word.
> Prayer is talking to God and Jesus.
> God and Jesus listen to my prayers.
> The church is a happy, loving place.

4- AND 5-YEAR-OLDS

Are eager to learn

Think concretely   Playact experiences

Are becoming very social and are making friends at church

Have great imaginations and are creative

Are wiggly but are learning to sit still

Like to explore and are curious

Learn by doing

Relate to the world from their experiences

Love to please, especially adults

Like big words, and their vocabulary is growing fast

Are physically growing fast

Are rapidly developing coordination

Can be boisterous and noisy, but can learn limits

Love repetition and routine which give them security

Young Children Come Packaged With Many Things!

Illustrated by Lorraine Arthur

2- and 3-Year-Olds

LOTS OF LOVE
ENERGY
SHORT ATTENTION SPAN
THEIR OWN WORLD
WIGGLES
SELF-CENTEREDNESS
LOTS OF QUESTIONS
NO INHIBITIONS
TOUCHY HANDS
DETERMINATION

4- and 5-Year-Olds

EAGERNESS
DESIRE TO PLEASE
FRIENDLINESS
CURIOSITY
IMAGINATION
EXPLORATION
NOISE
CREATIVITY
WIGGLES
GROWING VOCABULARY

Spiritual Understanding

God made the world; He is powerful.

A miracle is something only God can do.

God is good and He loves me.

God can help me to be good.

God loves me all the time, no matter what!

God sent baby Jesus; He grew just like I am growing.

Jesus is God's Son, my friend, and He loves me.

Jesus can do miracles because He is God's Son.

Jesus helps and forgives others.

Jesus died on the cross, rose from the dead, and lives in Heaven.

The Bible is God's true Word about God and Jesus.

My church is a happy place to be.

God wants me to tell others about Jesus.

TEMPERAMENTS—GOD PUT THEM THERE!

All people, including children, have a basic temperament that needs to be understood and also trained.

Sanguines are fun-loving and playful.

Cholerics like taking charge and being in control.

Melancholics want order and perfection.

Phlegmatics are easy-going and may appear lazy.

How Do Children Learn?

With all five senses—seeing, hearing, touching, smelling, and telling

By imitating (their teacher most importantly)

Through repetition

With play   As they make choices

Rule of Thumb Ratios

Substitute any age (1-5 years) in these ratios to ensure age-appropriate teaching.

A. Age to attention span: 4 years/4 minutes

B. Age to ability: 4 years/4 steps, materials, or facts

C. Age to number of
   children per teacher: 4 years/4 children per teacher

THE WELCOME

"Anyone who welcomes a little child like this in my name is welcoming me, and anyone who welcomes me is welcoming my Father who sent me!"

(Mark 9:37, *TLB*).

Protect yourself and your children with a security check-in and check-out system. Provide three security tags for each child. A simple numbering system works well as do permanent name tags. Ask the parent to pin one tag on the child, pin one on the diaper bag (birth-2 years), and keep one for pickup identification.

Develop a registration form or card. Gather helpful information, such as name, address, telephone number, birth date, parents' names, names of those in the household, special needs (i.e., allergies, disabilities), names of people who may pick up the child.

Identify teachers and helpers with name tags, aprons, or smocks.

Name tags for children will help teachers and helpers to easily call children by name. Use adhesive labels for young children. Older children will enjoy shapes cut from colorful paper, felt, or oilcloth. Add the child's schedule and special needs to the tag.

Name tags for children up to two years of age should be placed on the children's backs. Place tags on the fronts of children age three and up.

Make your check-in system short and sweet.

Provide a weekly parent sign-in sheet for children's names and parents' locations in case parents must be contacted by a helper or teacher.

Develop and publicize a policy for not accepting sick children.

Schedule greeters to:
  A. Assist with visitor and new member registration.
  B. Make children and parents feel welcome, secure, and familiar.
  C. Give newcomers and "reluctants" attention and reassurance.
  D. Direct children to learning centers or activities by explaining choices.

Provide coat hooks at the child's level and cubbyholes for storing belongings and take-home papers. Personalize hooks and cubbyholes so that children can identify their own. Use photos, pictures, colors, stickers, shapes, letters, or first names. Sheets from seasonal thematic note pads also can make good labels. Don't forget to provide a special section for visitors and newcomers.

Create cubbyholes from shoe organizers, ice cream tubs, or detergent boxes.

Let children and parents do as much as possible before entering the room.

Respect other children by having parents say good-bye at the door. Reassure parents and offer to take a reluctant child. Be quick with a smile and slow with the child.

Remove criers from the doorway. Express sad feelings back to the child. "It's sad to say good-bye." Comfort, distract, and attempt to get the child involved.

Remember that first impressions happen only once.

Teaching starts when the first child enters the room. Teaching stops when the last child leaves—or does it ever stop?

THE PROGRAM

"Those who plan what is good find love and faithfulness" (Proverbs 14:22, *NIV*).

Remember these five P's for a successful program:

Prayer—go to the source for guidance.

Planning—use varied resources.

Preparation—before class and setup.

Punctuality—says, "You're important. I'm here and ready."

Placement—who's where, when, and why?

LEARNING CENTERS

Use this rule: If activity ingredients are wet, use them on a table. If they are dry, place them on the floor.

Avoid clogged glue bottles. Cut an egg carton apart, leaving two cups together. Barely cover the bottom of one cup with glue and place two cotton sticks in the other. Place one pair of cups between every two children. No cleanup is needed; just throw away.

For water play, cover tables with bath towels. Use items to pour, funnel, mix, and pump. (Make a pump by cutting the bottom from a hand-pump soap bottle.)

Make butcher aprons from old oilcloth tablecloths, using bias tape or ribbon ties. The teacher should wear an apron around water or paint too.

Set up portable hand-washing areas. Cut a shower curtain into pieces to use under dishpans. Add motel soap, little sponges, old hand towels, and an inch or two of water.

Place a shower curtain or oilcloth on the floor under sand, soil, rice, beans, corn, or cornmeal. Lift sides and funnel the contents into a container when finished. Play with these dry ingredients with scoops, berry baskets, funnels, and measuring cups. Store everything in an old suitcase that lies flat.

Create "doctor play." Buy a painter mask. Tear a white sheet into strips for bandages. Provide a clipboard and toy telephone. Cut the collar off an old white shirt. Wear the shirt backwards and glue a red felt cross over the heart. Use the collar as a nurse's cap.

Activities should grow with the child. For instance, let a child begin pounding with a wooden peg bench, then try pounding golf tees into Styrofoam with a wooden hammer. Advance to a real hammer and nails to actually build something.

Place nature items on cotton in greeting card boxes with plastic covers. Tape or glue in items that are especially fragile. This allows children to observe without damaging.

Fill empty food boxes (i.e., gelatin, cereal, macaroni and cheese) with paper and cover with clear adhesive paper. This makes them sturdy and permanent for home living grocery play.

Use classroom bulletin boards as learning centers. Children will be more attracted to them if they participate in putting them together or can manipulate them in some way.

CLEANUP TIME

Cleanup time is a teaching time! Schedule time for it.

Involve children in cleanup. Mark plastic squirt bottles, "water only." Limit children to three squirts each, and let them scrub and clean the classroom.

Choose a helper to ring the "five more minutes" bell at each center.

Use the same signal (i.e., song, tape, xylophone) for cleanup time each week. This gives routine and allows independence. Children will say, "Oh, I know what that means."

Identifiable containers and locations make instructions clear to children. "Tony, please put the cars in the green box. Bethany, please put the people in the blue box." Enamel spray paint is cheap!

Divide large jobs into small jobs.

Make cleanup a game. "Joe, you be the road grader and push all the blocks over here for Anna to put away."

Have specific places for storing toys and supplies so they always go back to "their homes."

Learning starts early in life. Don't do for children what they can do for themselves.

Toddlers love to put and take; let them put their toys away.

Be consistent in your expectations.

Sing your directions by using familiar tunes. Sing, "Time to put the toys away" to the tune of "Mary Had a Little Lamb."

Each teacher should supervise her ratio of children (i.e., two 2-year-olds, three 3-year-olds, four 4-year-olds, five 5-year-olds). All children can help. Say, "Jesus was a helper and so am I."

Watch for opportunities to encourage and acknowledge children's efforts.

Admire the tidy room. Mention specific children and the jobs they did. Relate their work to the lesson emphasis (i.e., obey, good work, helper, kind).

Snack Time

Snack time is a teaching time!

Post a snack sign-up sheet for parents with dates, number in the class, and the time you serve snacks.

Drink water. It's not sticky!

Even a 2-year-old can put a napkin on the table by each chair. Place cups and napkins where young helpers can easily reach one at a time. Older children can distribute napkins and cups from a small bucket they carry.

Use ball caps, signs on yarn necklaces, or stickers to identify helpers.

Emphasize sharing, helping, and taking turns during snack time. Choose helpers by writing names on a chart or placing names on index cards and placing them in a spray-painted adhesive strip can. Children are reassured of "their" turn if they know "their" names are on the list.

Fill small water pitchers half full, and give instructions to fill cups half full. Keep towels handy. Lead children to clean up spills.

Encourage children to wait for their snacks with "hands behind your backs." This eliminates spills and eating before prayer time.

Use snack time to encourage each child to respond with a "Yes, please" or "No, thank you" when they are offered food or drink.

As children begin to finish snack time and cleanup time, turn out the lights and have them rest their heads on the table. During this quiet relief period you will be able to see who is ready for the next activity.

Tips for Teachers—Early Childhood

Snack time is a very tangible time for prayer. Encourage the child praying out loud to use a loud voice, "Like the preacher's."

Cleanup helpers can be chosen, or let each child throw his own trash away and return to his seat. This offers limited and directed movement with few directions.

TRANSITION TIMES

Transition times are teaching times!

Plan well and plan ahead. If you fail to plan, you plan to fail.

Use a light flicker, bell, piano notes, or song to get the children's attention.

Give simple, specific directions so that children understand what is expected. Remember the age ratio: the number of instruction steps should be equal to or less than the child's age. (See page 10.)

Keep children gathered and focused by moving immediately to the next activity. If you don't have something ready they'll find something!

Smooth transitions give a sense of security. When children feel things are out of control, they are out of control!

One teacher should always be ready to direct the class while others participate with the children.

If you have a Sunday school time followed by a worship time when children come and go, a greeter can help facilitate the "coming" and "going" between these hours. Plan activities that will allow arriving children to be added and children leaving to drop out. Some suggestions follow.

Pretend!
A. Get a balloon or bubble gum out of your pocket. Blow, blow, blow. Clap hands when it pops. Peel gum off your face. Wrap it in paper; throw it away.
B. Lie on your back and look up at the sky. See the cloud shapes, stars, and moon. Look into a tree. See leaves, monkeys, birds, Zacchaeus.

Cut snowflakes from used fabric softener sheets or clouds from leftover cotton batting. Hold them and move to the music of "Dance of the Sugar Plum Fairy," "Grand Canyon Suite," or other music with speed and sound variations.

Make a "feely box" by cutting two holes in a large box. Allow children to reach in and guess what they feel. Place enough items related to the story or season inside, so many turns can be taken.

Play with rhythm sticks. Lay two sticks parallel, crisscross, or in a T shape. Say, "Make yours look like mine." Allow children to lead while others follow. Tap out children's names or Bible words, and, of course, march to music. "Watch the director. Tap high, tap low, tap front, tap back."

Play games, such as Musical Chairs; Red Light, Green Light; Duck, Duck, Goose; Mother, May I?

BIBLE TIME

Preparation

Check the atmosphere. Do the children have wiggles? Is it a good time to pray or introduce the story? Don't waste God's Word if nobody's ready.

What does the lesson say to you? Apply it to your personal life.

Read the Scripture from different versionsof the Bible. Know the story background and setting, the facts, and the framework.

Remember the ratios? (See page 10.) Choose the number of facts that equal the child's age and present them in the number of minutes that equal the child's age. What four things do you want to emphasize with 4-year-olds in four minutes?

Practice with visuals. Will they work with your class size? Real items make the story more alive and memorable.

Read the story from children's story books. Think action, people, repetitious words, dialogue, sound effects, feelings.

Review your lesson the evening before or earlier in the day. Yes, teaching takes planning, scheduling, and effort.

You may be the only Bible a child will ever "read."

Identify the large group area with a masking tape circle, carpet samples, pillows, or strips of colored cloths for each small group. (Make colored cloths with six-yard strips of colorful, washable material. Fold them smaller for small groups.)

Use a low table or cabinet for the Bible, teaching picture, visuals, and tape recorder. Keep your flannelgraph board in this area and a chair to help make the teacher visible, if you have more than ten to twelve children.

Children should face the teacher and the teacher should face the door.

Remove wiggles with fingerplays and songs. This also gives helpers an opportunity to position themselves for quiet control while continuing to participate.

A. I'll reach up to the ceiling (arms up),
   I'll stretch out to the wall (arms in front).
   I'll bend to touch my knees and toes,
   And sit down very small.
B. Make a little tiny bed and tuck those wiggles right in before the Bible story.
C. Tune: "The Farmer in the Dell"
   I have two listening ears (repeated four times).

Have you planned for the class to taste, touch, smell, hear, and see the story or Bible truth?

Explain listening guidelines, or let children take turns giving them as they learn and understand them.

A. Hands—on your own body.
(Yes, anywhere. Sometimes we just can't hold them still in our laps.)

B. Ears—listen.

C. Eyes—look at the teacher.
(Are you at the child's eye level? Can all children see you and the visuals you may use?)

D. Bottoms—flat on the floor.
(Lying on tummies puts our feet in someone's face, or toes may start tapping on the floor.)

E. Mouth—zip it, tape it, lock it, snap it.
(Don't ask a question after this is done. It's hard to talk with your mouth zipped!)

Plan to alternate active times with quiet times, large muscle activities with small muscle activities, and times when the teacher talks with turns for children to talk. Remember the attention span ratio: a child's age is equal to his attention span in minutes. (See page 10.)

Start early—this Sunday night for next Sunday morning is good. Pray.

Concentrate so hard on the children that you forget all about the adults and yourself.

Have the children act out action parts.
"Samuel was asleep." (Lie down.)
"He heard a voice." (Sit up, putting hand to ear.)
"He walked into Eli's room." (Stand up and walk in place.)

"What's in my sack?" can be used to introduce the lesson. Place an object relating to the story or the lesson aim in a paper sack. Let the children take turns guessing what is in the sack. They will watch and listen intently to see what's inside.

Tell the Bible story like you believe it. If people walk, walk your fingers or your legs; if someone listens, pause and put your hand to your ear; if they look, shade eyes and look around the room. Simply act out the action words.

Let the people talk to each other. Raise and lower your voice. Count out numbers. (Well, maybe not forty days and forty nights!) Repeat phrases.

Describe the environment. "It was a chilly, dark night. The wind blew water in their faces." (Have someone flicker the lights and squirt water overhead.) Or, "The sun and sand were very hot. Ouch!"

With a Bible on your lap, focus on the children, depend on the Lord, and enjoy yourself.

Look the children in the eyes. Pull them into the story action with your eyes, your voice, and your body. Lean forward; lean backward; look up.

Stop when the story ends!

REVIEW AND RETELL

Compliment the children on being good listeners. Let them "unzip" their mouths.

Use, sparingly, questions with yes, no, God, or Jesus answers.

Use what, where, and when questions according to age ratios(i.e., 2 years/2 questions, 3 years/3 questions, 4 years/4 questions, 5 years/5 questions). For older children, or at the end of the year, try how and why questions. They are harder and more abstract.

Try to involve all children. "If you know what swallowed Jonah, put your hands on your knees. If you know where Jesus saw Zacchaeus, put your finger on your nose."

Be sensitive to the time it takes for some young children to respond. You may need to restate the question.

Having a child stand by you with your arm around him helps him feel secure in answering questions.

Help the child answer successfully. Rephrase the question or ask something simpler. Whisper the answer if necessary.

Hand out visuals. Lead children to tell you something they know about the story. "Tell me what person you have. What did he do?"

Ask, "What do you see in this picture? What can you tell me about the picture?"

Use a puppet for children to hold and answer questions or retell the story.

Children absorb more than they can give back. If you do your part, God will give the increase. (Read 1 Corinthians 3:6, 7.)

BIBLE WORDS AND SONGS

Sing Bible words to a familiar tune. Sing, "Do that which is right and good" to the tune of "Jesus Loves Me," or go up and down a musical scale with the verse.

Clap out verses one word at a time or follow words with a double clap. "I will (clap/clap) follow (clap/clap) the example (clap/clap) of Christ (clap/clap). First Corinthians (clap/clap) eleven (clap/clap), verse 1 (clap/clap)."

Post words to songs behind the teacher for substitutes and parent helpers.

Explain unfamiliar words. Ask children for meanings, such as "What does selfish mean?" (Young children may think it means a big fish in the ocean with a sail on its back!) A little girl requested her favorite song, "Let's sing the witch song!" She wanted to sing, "Do That Which Is Right and Good."

Use a wind-up musical toy to sing with. These are short, simple, and familiar songs. Look for electronic music boxes in craft stores. Children can take turns pushing the button as you sing.

Learn songs used in adult worship. Children will be glad when they can sing along to familiar choruses, such as "Oh, How I Love Jesus," "Jesus Loves Even Me," and "This Is the Day." Listen for songs with repetition and tunes that you go home humming.

Use the tunes to familiar hymns and change the words.

    A. Tune: "More About Jesus"
       Tell, tell about Jesus,
       Tell, tell about Jesus;
       Tell of His loving caring ways,
       Tell of His love for you and me.

    B. Tune: "I Would Be Like Jesus"
       Be like Jesus, this my song,
       In my home, I won't do wrong;
       Be like Jesus, all day long!
       I will be like Jesus.

Children like variety. Learn a new song each week or at least each month. Listen to the song over and over while you are doing activities. Then concentrate on the words during circle time.

> You may say, "I can't sing." Neither can most preschoolers, at least not very well. If you can't sing it, say it, or "Make a joyful noise unto the Lord" (Psalm 98:4). He will honor your effort!

PRAYER TIME

Prayer time is all the time!

Praying is talking to a real God who listens. Look for opportunities to pray spontaneously. "God, You made a beautiful sun." "God, help me to share with John." "God, thank You for my friends."

> Young children can learn to praise God, petition God for themselves and others, and thank God.

Help children realize answers to their prayers, such as needs being met, safe travel, missionary friends' needs, and a new building.

> Use pictures to help children identify prayer needs and praises.

Pray at specific times—before the Bible story, at snack time, for playground safety, and before you say good-bye.

> Give children opportunities to pray.

When we work, we work. When we pray, God works.

COMMUNICATION—
ATTENTION AND AFFIRMATION

"Let your conversation be always full of grace, seasoned with salt, so that you may know how to answer everyone" (Colossians 4:6, *NIV*).

WITH CHILDREN

Call the children by name. That means learning them quickly by studying your class list. Pray for them by name.

Focus on the children. Get down on their level physically, and it will help you be there verbally.

Control the enthusiastic, include the quiet, limit the talker, touch the tactile, and provide movement for the wiggler.

Ask open-ended questions. Ask, "How did the shepherds find baby Jesus?" rather than, "Did the shepherds find baby Jesus?"

Smile freely—that says a lot!

Communicate love and acceptance with appropriate touches—hugs, pats on backs, tousling hair, and holding hands.

Acknowledge and accept feelings. Approach a reluctant child cautiously, but don't give up.

Speak slowly, quietly, and simply.

Be very generous with praise and encouragement. Affirm any attempt at creating, helping, or listening. Let children overhear you praising them to others.

> **C**ompliments are more valuable when focused on what the child does, rather than on clothing, looks, or other intangibles.

Young children are very literal. If Jesus wants them to be "fishers of men," they wonder what kind of pole and hook to use. Explanations are always in order.

> **B**reak large tasks into small, specific jobs. Cleanup, snack time, and good-bye time can be overwhelming if not directed carefully.

State expectations in a positive way. Say what to do, rather than what not to do. "Feet are for walking." "Use a soft singing voice." "Carry the chair in front of you." "Tables are for working; the floor and chairs are for sitting."

> **T**ry to use words that are think starters, not think stoppers? Say, "Where do we keep our papers?" rather than, "Put your papers in the cubbyholes."

Make a friend. Communicate by mail with even regular attenders. Use extra activity sheets, take-home papers, art projects, or postcards. Put in a sticker, gum, or snapshot of a class activity.

Nonverbal communication—body position, facial expression, hurried or relaxed attitude, voice tone—speaks loudly, too!

Help with other church activities where you will see or work with your class members, such as special occasion child care, children's programs, parties, or summer events.

WITH HOME/PARENTS

Introduce yourself to parents with a letter or open house at promotion time. Parents will not feel they are leaving their child with a complete stranger.

Post a list of staff and staff needs, a class schedule, Bible learning centers, upcoming activities, and class snapshots outside the classroom.

Plan a parent's meeting where the methods and goals of your class are explained. Teach them the children's favorite songs and Bible verses.

Let parents sign up as classroom helpers. Inform them of the lesson aim, Bible story, the center they will help in, and other helper expectations. A parent helper letter is helpful to clarify this information.

Take time to telephone and introduce yourself to parents. Ask if they have any questions or comments. Update any registration information.

Visit in the home. This is almost a lost art, but it is still the best way for the parents to know you and for you to know the child. Call ahead for a convenient time. Keep your visit short and simple. Take something for the child to do while you visit, and ask the child to show you something special that belongs to him.

Send a thank-you letter at the end of the year, before promotion. Encourage the parents to become involved in church activities and attend a Bible study.

WITH CHILDREN WITH DISABILITIES

Rationale: A trend in the care of children with disabilities is early intervention. The earlier the child's needs are addressed, the better. The church as well should provide services early in the life of the child.

If there are young children with disabilities in your group, include them. Making them a part of the age-appropriate class now will make acceptance more natural later. Obtain information about the specific diagnosis and ask parents for essential information about their care.

Prepare children without disabilities for the experience. Brief, simple explanations are adequate: "Our friend, Joey, has cerebral palsy. The words mean that his brain was hurt and he can't walk and run as you can. What he says isn't always clear. He is a nice boy and wants to learn about Jesus just as much as you do." Read to the class the children's book, *Just Like Everybody Else* (Pierson, Jim. Cincinnati: Standard Publishing, 1993).

Be aware that most children with disabilities will need more room to move around. Accessible rest rooms, wide doors, ramps, and grab bars offer security. Make the classroom safe. Cover sharp edges.

Special seating for the child will not be a problem. Because the youngster needs it all of the time, his family will bring it with him. If special equipment is not available, ask an adult class or group to purchase it.

Record emergency information about the child. Are there allergies? Does he choke easily? How does he communicate his needs, especially for toileting? Does he have significant fears? Does he wander?

Use a variety of teaching methods to stimulate the five senses—seeing, hearing, touching, smelling, and tasting. Children of all abilities will profit from this approach.

Young children don't notice differences. If they do, the differences aren't important to them. Watch them react to their disabled classmates. They can teach adults a lot of important lessons on acceptance.

THE ROOM—
PHYSICAL CARE AND ARRANGEMENT

"In my Father's house are many rooms; if it were not so, I would have told you. I am going there to prepare a place for you"   (John 14:2, *NIV*).

The relationship, not the room, is the key to John 14:2.

Sit on the floor in the middle of your room and take a "child's-eye view" of the surroundings. Does your room look loved and say, "I love you; come in and learn"?

Check up, clean up, fix up, paint up!

Things to remember: heat rises, sun glares, drafts chill, still is stuffy.

Clean carpet is warm and comfortable. Cover carpet with a shower curtain for "messy" projects. Have one available for each hour. Take curtains home (along with paint aprons) and machine wash on gentle cycle.

Children need their space. Twenty-five to thirty feet per child is best.

Tables should be elbow high when children are sitting. Small tables are better for movement and space than large tables.

If furniture inhibits child movement, move it out. If you need more child space, think: off the floor, up on walls, out the door. Substitute a xylophone for a piano, a retractable clothesline for a drying rack, hooks for home living clothes in place of floor shelves.

Children's feet should touch the floor when they sit in chairs. Try to keep all adult furniture out of the early childhood area. (The exception would be the rocking chairs in the infant room.)

Plan a specific time for "spring" housecleaning—after VBS, before promotion day, or a half-hour at monthly meetings—or let staff and parents select their own time and project.

Divide and conquer. Make a list of sorting, cleaning, fixing, and filing. If you cannot sort and throw out, choose a person to help you, and "close your eyes."

Use the children to help keep the room tidy. Sand splintered blocks; wash dolls, clothes, dishes, cars, animals, clay tools, puzzle pieces; discard dried up markers; sort crayons. Plan this as a learning center activity.

Uniform storage boxes (i.e., computer paper, boot or shoe) save space and stack nicely.

Everybody's job is nobody's job. Assign specific tasks.

Paint storage boxes to match walls, if shelves are open. Label with large, clear lettering. Use a computer to letter labels, or type and enlarge them with a photocopier. Tape or rubber cement labels to boxes.

Label a large box for each season. Store reusable bulletin board pieces, visuals, and quarterly teaching pictures.

Give ownership of a classroom to all who use it by giving opportunity for room TLC.

ARRANGE FOR ACTIVITY

Keep a greeting area clear for "coming" and "going" activity.

Use the block area for large group activities. Both take up and need ample space.

Place water play at the end of a rectangular table rather than in the center of a round or trapezoid table.

The teacher should sit where she can assist the children easily without getting up. This keeps the teacher at the children's eye level.

Keep compatible activities together. Books and puzzles are quiet. Blocks and family living tend to be busy.

Tips for Teachers—Early Childhood

Put tossing games against a wall for a natural boundary.

Arrange the art center near water, cabinets, and supplies.

Family living, music, and large group times need electrical plugs near by. Use safety covers when not in use.

Plan for safety when you cook. Use ample table space. Unplug appliances immediately. Stay between the cooking utensils and children. An electric oven should be within reach of the teacher only.

DECORATE AND EDUCATE

Well-tended live plants give opportunity for praise, and show there is life and that someone cares.

If you move tables for learning centers, mark original locations with large ceiling decorations (i.e., autumn leaves, happy faces, snowflakes, flowers). Children can help replace them for snack and story times.

Test dabs of rubber cement or masking tape (two inch pieces folded into a circle with the sticky side out) to see if residue will rub off walls before attaching large pictures or art work.

To make a picture board, cover an 8 ½" x 11" piece of construction paper with clear adhesive paper. Cut it into four equal (2 ¾" x 8 ½") strips. Trim a piece of cardboard to be the same size as your teaching pictures. Angle a strip of covered construction paper across each corner of the cardboard. Fold back ends and glue to the back. Place a picture in the picture board.

Children can handle pictures easily in picture boards (see above). Pass them in a circle. Mount them in learning centers at the children's eye level. Hold them for the group to see. Lay them on the floor. Take turns tossing a bean bag and telling about the picture the bag lands on.

Let children decorate adding machine tape to use as bulletin board borders. Use stamp pads, sponge paints, stickers, or markers.

Place nature items on windowsills. Change with lessons and seasons.

Plan a place for everything and put everything in its place.

CLASSROOM MANAGEMENT

"Everything should be done in a fitting and orderly way"
(1 Corinthians 14:40, *NIV*).

TEACHERS, HELPERS, AND SUBSTITUTES

Send thank-you notes to your substitute every time. "Glad you were here" postcards work nicely. It's OK to be brief, but be sincere.

Substitutes are potential teachers. Be looking and praying for someone with whom you would like to work. Every teacher is a recruiter!

Ask parents to be a class time helper, bring snacks, plan parties or activities, or share a skill or special information with your class.

A substitute teacher with children hanging all over her was known to say, "I was called to be a sub for an emergency a year ago. Have they found a teacher yet?" Protect and honor the commitment of a substitute.

Never leave children unsupervised. Take them all with you if necessary.

If an activity is not working, adapt, redirect, change. Be flexible.

Be in your room and ready, to allow time for parents to be on time for their worship service or class.

Keeping your door closed until fifteen or twenty minutes before class time gives you opportunity to set up and to pray. People will respect your preparation time if they are informed.

Have an emergency evacuation plan posted and be sure parents are informed.

Count children every time you move from one room to another.

CHILDREN

After forming a circle for games, have children put their hands on their knees or sides. This prevents tugging and pulling.

Allow children to choose a center, but limit the number of children at each center at a given time by limiting chairs or materials. Children may then stay at a center as long as they wish if it does not keep another child from having a turn. Encourage them to try all areas.

Expect children to finish puzzles, throw away scraps, pick up around their chairs, return aprons after washing their hands, put papers in their cubbyholes, and complete any other personal cleanup.

Give children a minimum of help to maximize their independent growth.

When moving 2- and 3-year-olds outside the classroom for walks, or rest-room or playground visits, use a rope with knotted loops about twelve inches apart. Lead the rope while each child holds onto a loop. Have older children walk in single file to avoid tugging and pulling. Pretend to be a train, plane, or animal. Tiptoe or skate.

Wagon rides in the hallway help give toddlers variety.

Teach children to walk on the right side of the hall by running their right hands along the wall. Explain this act of respect and courtesy to the children.

Children like to please, so give them responsibilities. Try to match assigned tasks to the child's abilities and interests. Don't expect perfection.

Keep all children involved in games. Keep them in the circle or let them take turns helping with the music. "You're out" games do not work well with young children.

Allow opportunities for being with friends and making choices during learning center and snack times.

Most children know colors but cannot read. Make color-coded happy face buttons for each teacher and child. Group children by color groups to walk in the halls together and sit together for Bible time and small group activities. Colored pillows can help identify each group's space. Make eight to twelve inch pillows in primary colors in the shape of squares, triangles, circles, and rectangles.

SUPPLIES

Keep glue, scissors, crayons, and markers in hospital washtubs or other small containers. (Stand markers and crayons in plastic cups before placing them in tubs.) Take the tubs to centers and allow children to help clean up.

Leftover stickers can be sorted by categories and used in learning centers.

Keep adhesive strips for minor cuts and scratches.

Cover items children will not be using. They will want an opportunity to use what they can see. Use a curtain to cover shelves.

Submit bills marked "Donation" for the little things you buy for your room. It gives your leader an accurate picture of the value of the early childhood area.

Ask a helper to prepare your activity sheets by sorting them into lessons, dividing them into groups, and placing them in plastic storage bags. Place bags in file folders marked with lesson numbers.

Use extra take-home papers to mail to absentees, let children take to friends, give to a child care center, or send to a mission.

DISCIPLINE

"Train a child in the way he should go, and when he is old he will not turn from it" (Proverbs 22:6, *NIV*).

The goal of discipline is inner control versus outward control. It is a process to teach children self-control and character-building.

Use your best resources:
  A. God's principles
  B. Jesus' love
  C. The Holy Spirit's guidance

Evaluate the situation first, not the child:
  A. Are the five P's of teaching in place—prayer, planning, preparation, punctuality, and placement? (See page 14.)
  B. Have you learned the children's names?
  C. Did you have the children's attention before giving directions?
  D. What in your classroom may be causing the problem? Move it, cover it, or offer it at another time.
  E. Do you offer variety?
  F. Do the children know they will each have a turn?
  G. Have you made the children wait?
  H. Can they see and hear?
  I. Are they comfortable? (Think of Goldilocks! Too hot, too cold, too big, too little, too full, too empty?)
  J. When do most of the problems happen?

Never embarrass a child.

Work with your teaching team on solutions. A little girl always seemed disruptive when she arrived the second hour. Her exuberant greeting of the other children did not always fit with the transition game. Simply changing this time to snack time allowed the social butterfly to greet and visit without interrupting.

> Direct your discipline at the behavior, not the child. The child always must be accepted, even when the behavior is not.

Discipline should teach, help, and love.

> Never force a child to say, "I'm sorry." He may not be!

Never make comparisons. Encourage self-improvement.

> Be calm, positive, and quiet in your conversation.

Pleasing requests get better results than demanding orders. Which do you like to hear?
"You may throw your scraps away."
"Pick up your scraps and throw them away."
"Please sit flat in your chair."
"Keep those chair legs on the floor."

> Try to get the child's cooperation and participation by having him explain the problem.

Explain to a child that his actions may hurt others. One biter did not know this and seemed sadder than the one he had bitten.

Let your touch be with love. A rub on the back speaks loudly to a restless child.

Set guidelines that a child can understand and follow and that teachers know and keep. Think about safety, care of property, respect for others.

Natural consequences are the best punishment for unacceptable behavior. If blocks are misused, remove the child from the block center. If a child runs in the hallway, insist that he begin again and walk. If a child bothers a friend, find him another place to sit or work.

Try distraction and redirection before you eliminate a child from an activity or the room.

Use a watching wall—an isolated wall that has no furniture, but where children can stand and watch the action. Observers need time to join in. Disrupters need to be separated until they can join in acceptably. Most children will be ready to join the group in one or two minutes. Reinvite but don't give excessive attention. Use several walls or places rather than putting children together; don't let it become a social outing for two buddies.

If there are young nonparticipators who just drop out and wander off, a helper should walk them back to the circle and help them get reinvolved.

The best discipline is self-discipline in prayer. Pray for yourself, your team, your children, and your program. Praise God for everything, even problems.

Use the child's nature to your advantage. Let the talker explain, pray, answer, and tell as much as possible.

Use a puppet to speak to each "good" child. Everyone will want to earn the puppet's greeting.

When a child is distracting and disrespectful, he is needing individual attention. A teacher or helper should walk him out of the classroom and reassure him that he is loved and cared for. If applicable, the child should be reassured of his parents' return and the class boundaries. Some children are very determined, so allow ample time to just sit and wait it out. Talk about pets, babies, brothers and sisters, trips, or anything that might strike a familiar cord and win you a friend.

When removing a child from the classroom, always stay in an open public area in the sight of other adults.

Consult your children's director or have a professional come and observe your classroom. Preschool directors or teachers, public school teachers, veteran Sunday school teachers, or even a grandmother may be able to give you some insights into handling a difficult child.

Always consider the child's safety, especially if you have an "escapee." Restrain the child with your arms completely around him until he relaxes or says he will stand with you.

Get to know parents early so they can be consulted about difficult, ongoing problems. Most are anxious for their children to have the best experience possible. Simply ask for any suggestions or information they can offer.

THE GOOD-BYE

"Go everywhere in the world. Tell the Good News to everyone"   (Mark 16:15, *ICB*).

Close the door before Bible time and open it when you are finished. Children will become used to the open door and will not associate it with parents coming. You can then see when parents start arriving and can stay with the children until then.

At check-out time, involve the children in an activity that will allow them to drop out as parents arrive. (See Transition Times, page 19.)

One or more teachers should be at the door to greet parents and ask the child's name or request a security identifier given at check-in time. Take your time. Most parents will be very patient.

Quietly (you're not a short-order cook) remove each child from the activity as parents arrive. Follow through, checking out one child at a time, to avoid confusion and forgotten take-home papers.

This can be a very anxious time for children if activity stops and everyone is waiting by the door. Keep children involved, preferably facing away from the door. Involved, interested children eliminate the chance of an anxious "escapee" or overly concerned parents.

The Good-bye

Be sensitive to parents' needs. There are special occasions when they must leave quickly.

Remove name tags and collect take-home papers. Help older children do these things themselves. It's slower, but it teaches. Having crafts and take-home papers in cubbyholes ahead of time makes the pickup time smoother.

For a safer, smoother check-out system, parents and family should remain in the hall.

Call each child by name as you say good-bye at the child's eye level. Good-byes are the last impression and should be pleasant.

Show excitement as you anticipate seeing the child next week. Hugs may be in order.

Insist that adults, rather than children or siblings, pick up and bring early childhood children. List authorized persons on the registration form and on the back of the name tag.

Suggest something from the lesson that children can tell to their families (i.e., a song, a name, an event).

Always be ready to share something positive about each child, such as "Tony was a good listener today." Remember, all the flowers of tomorrow are in the seeds of today!